#ManWisdom

Eric D Tokajer

MDN

P.O. Box 10943

Pensacola, Florida 32524

raveric@gmail.com

ISBN: 978-0-9894901-8-4

For my wife of 35 years
Pammy, without whom
I would know none
of what is contained
within this book.

Your wife can never
have too many shoes
or compliments.
But shoes cost more.

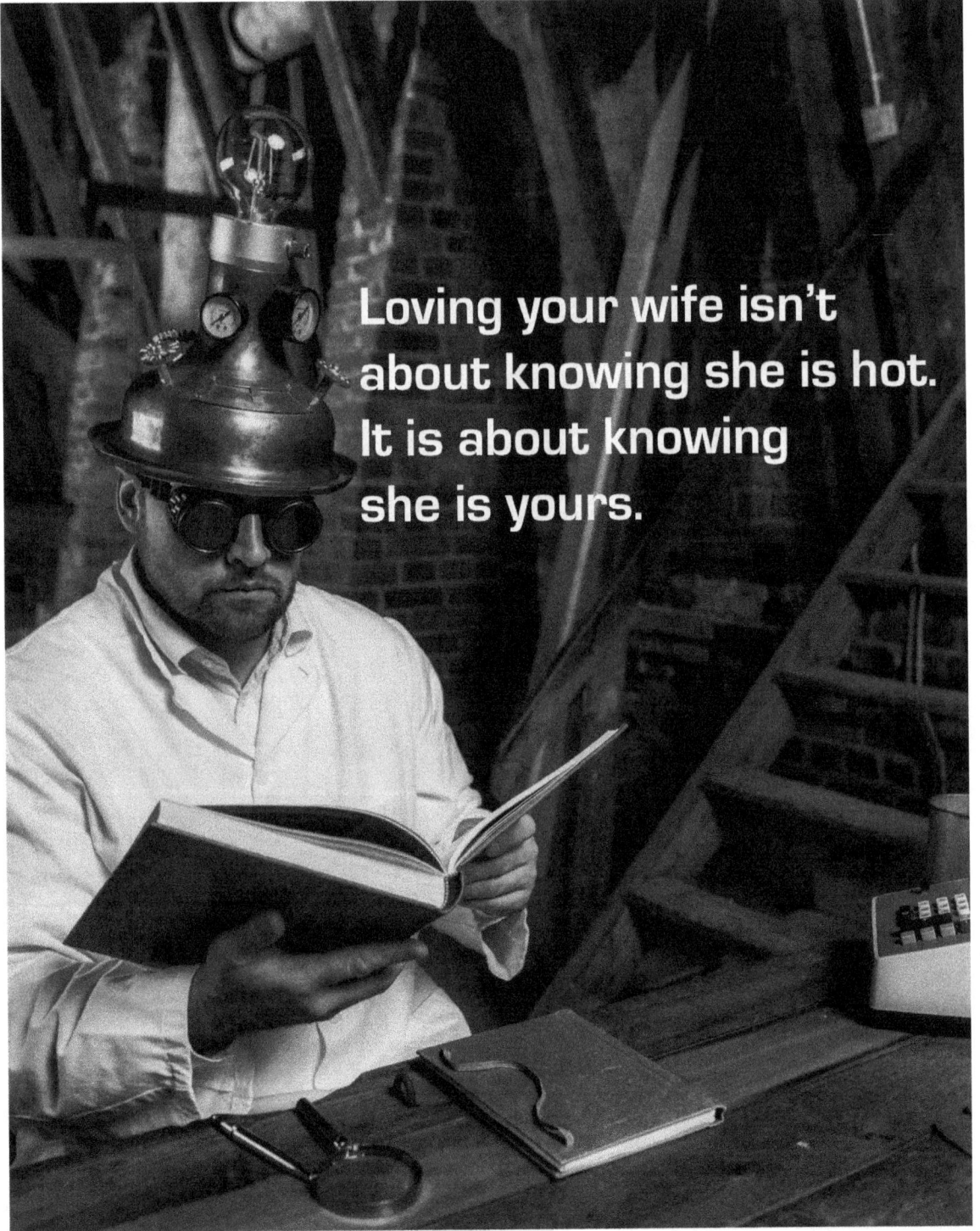

Loving your wife isn't about knowing she is hot. It is about knowing she is yours.

Before giving your wife spiritual directions make sure you have read the map.

Remember as you age,
a well taken care of
antique increases in
Value.

Your wife is not a ball
& chain, she is an anchor.
A ball & chain keeps you
from freedom, an anchor
keeps you safe in a storm.

Always season your words with grace, because your wife seasons your food.

If the only trip, you take your wife on, is a guilt trip, you are doing it wrong.

If you want your wife to act like the woman you dated... Keep dating her.

Never wait for a better time to say I love you, because it may never come.

Remember where you were when you first knew that you loved your wife, go there everyday in your mind.

No one should praise your wife more or defend her more strongly

You are not promised a tomorrow to be a better husband, make today count.

Always remember, that you cannot decide, what your wife's heart considers important.

Never let the fear of being viewed as weak keep you from being strong.

If you don't sow seeds of doubt, you won't grow roots of bitterness.

The best gift that you can give to your wife is your heart.

Just remember that a burnt meal is actually G-D encouraging you to take your wife out to dinner.

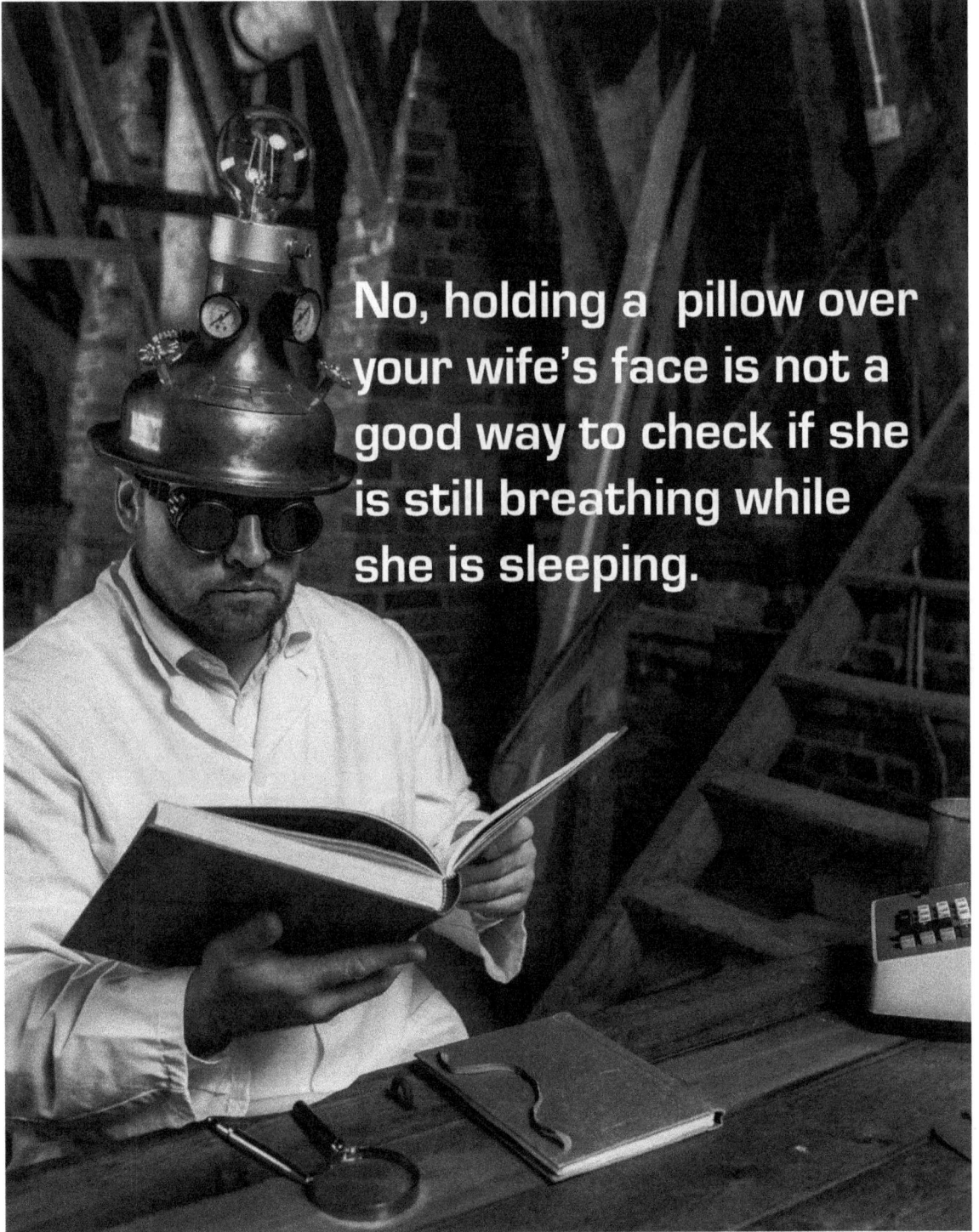

No, holding a pillow over your wife's face is not a good way to check if she is still breathing while she is sleeping.

Always remember we are to use things and love people, never the other way around.

If you answer any question with only one word, your wife will believe it is because you just don't want to talk to her.

Some men show more mercy for a ball team than they do for their wife.

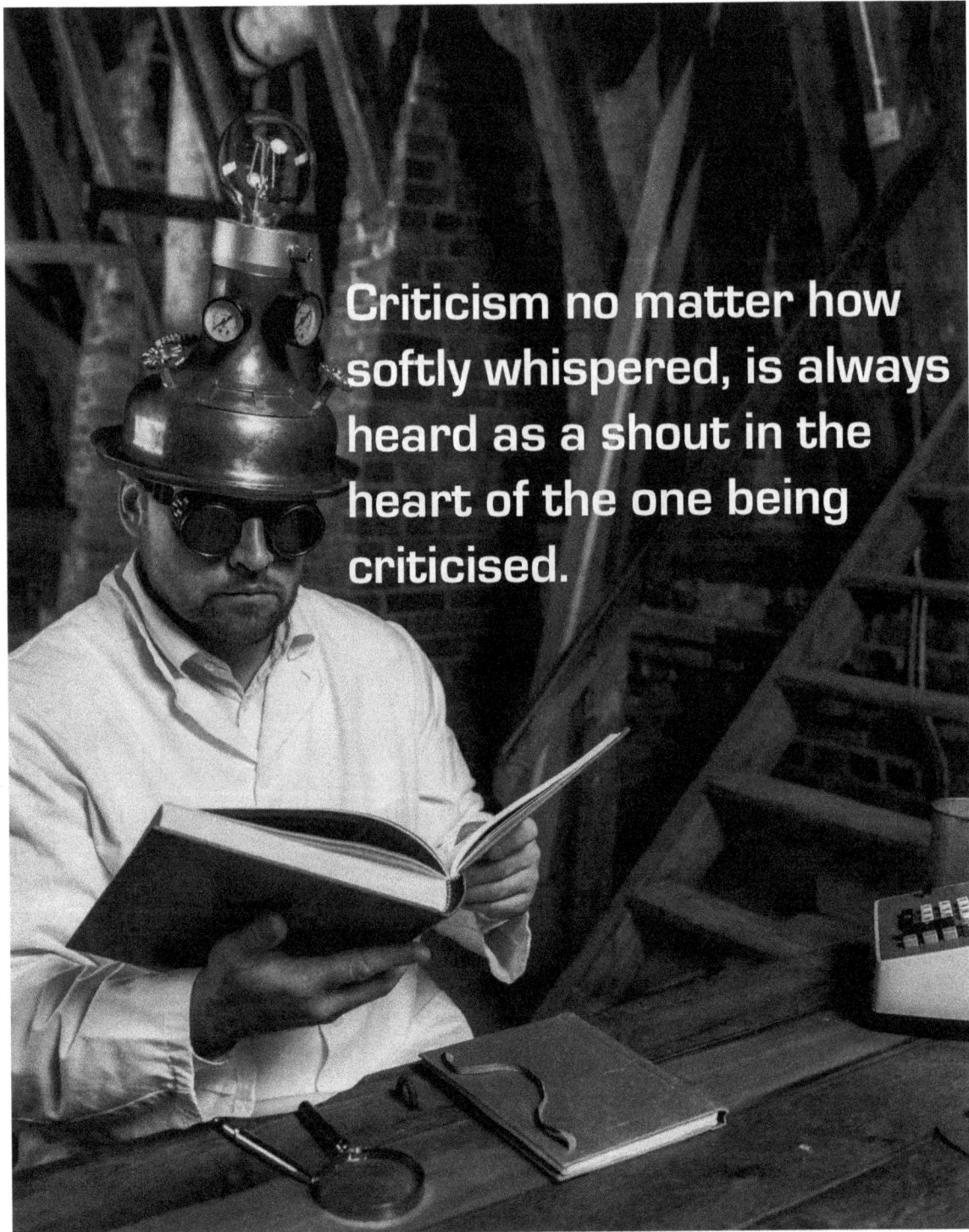

Criticism no matter how softly whispered, is always heard as a shout in the heart of the one being criticised.

Shallowness is only
helpful if you are trying
to cross a river.

Don't let the things you spend time doing for your wife, become a priority over actually spending time with your wife.

One of the best ways to say "I love you" to your wife, is by saying "what can I do for you today?"

Your wife's primary purpose is to help you, with you, not to help with other stuff.

When your wife says she doesn't care where you go for dinner, know assuredly this is not a statement of ambivalence, it is a test of your knowledge of her desires.

You cannot be the spiritual leader of your home, unless you are moving closer to G-D yourself.

Leave your wife a note or text her something sweet during the day, it will bless her to know she was on your mind.

Nothing makes a wife
feel more beautiful than
to have her husband
behave as if she is.

You can only realize the value of your wife when you see her as a gift from G-D. In other words if it was totally up to you, you couldn't afford the wife you have.

Your love for your wife can best be measured by your efforts to protect her spiritually, physically and emotionally.

If you want to be your wife's hero, think of the thing she has asked you to do for the hundredth time this week and do it.

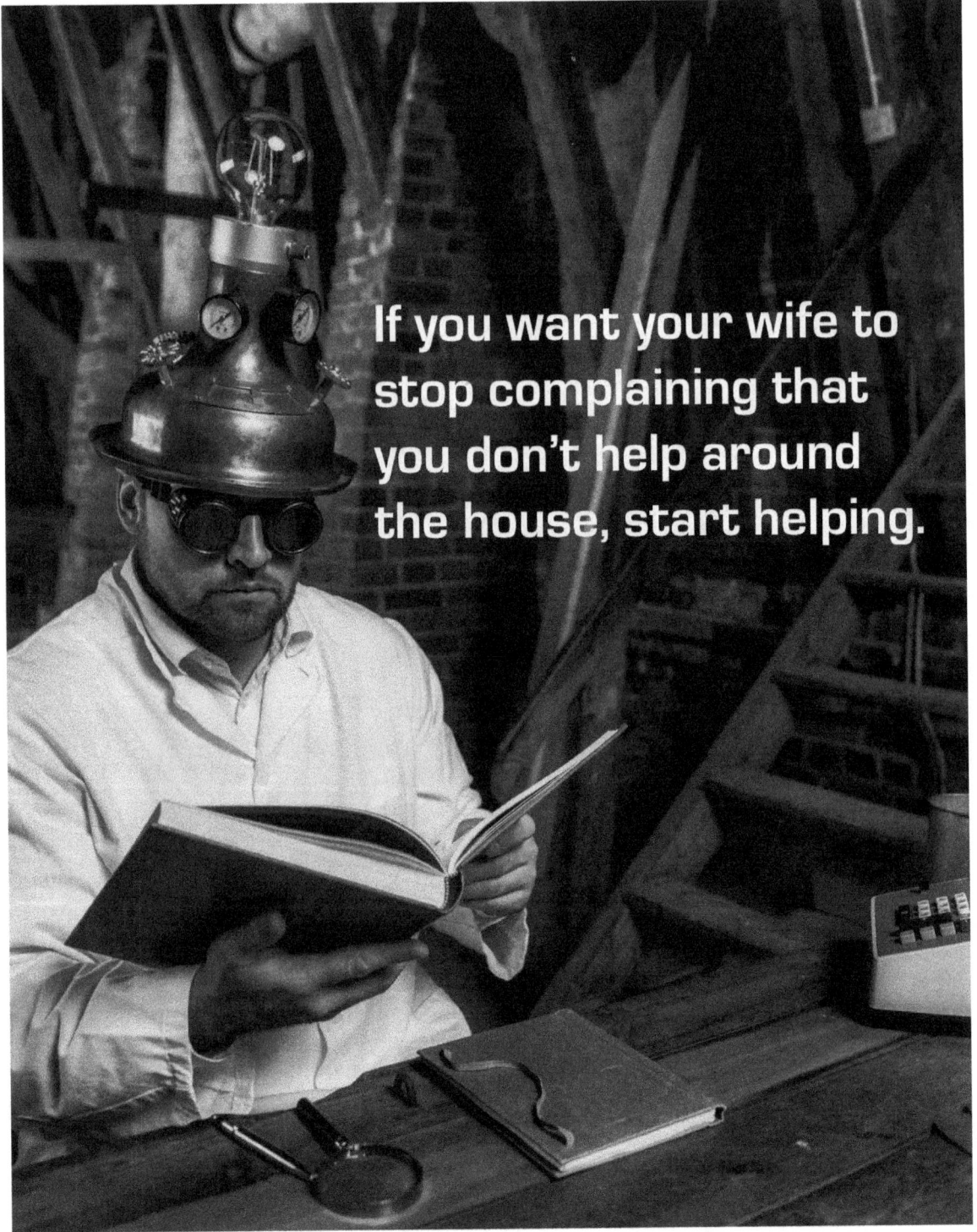

If you want your wife to stop complaining that you don't help around the house, start helping.

Listening to your wife when she speaks will dramatically increase the chances of your understanding what she is trying to tell you.

It doesn't matter how many times you remind your wife about something she forgot. It will not enable her to do it yesterday.

Your wife should be the princess in all of your dreams. And the majority of your dreams should take place while you are awake.

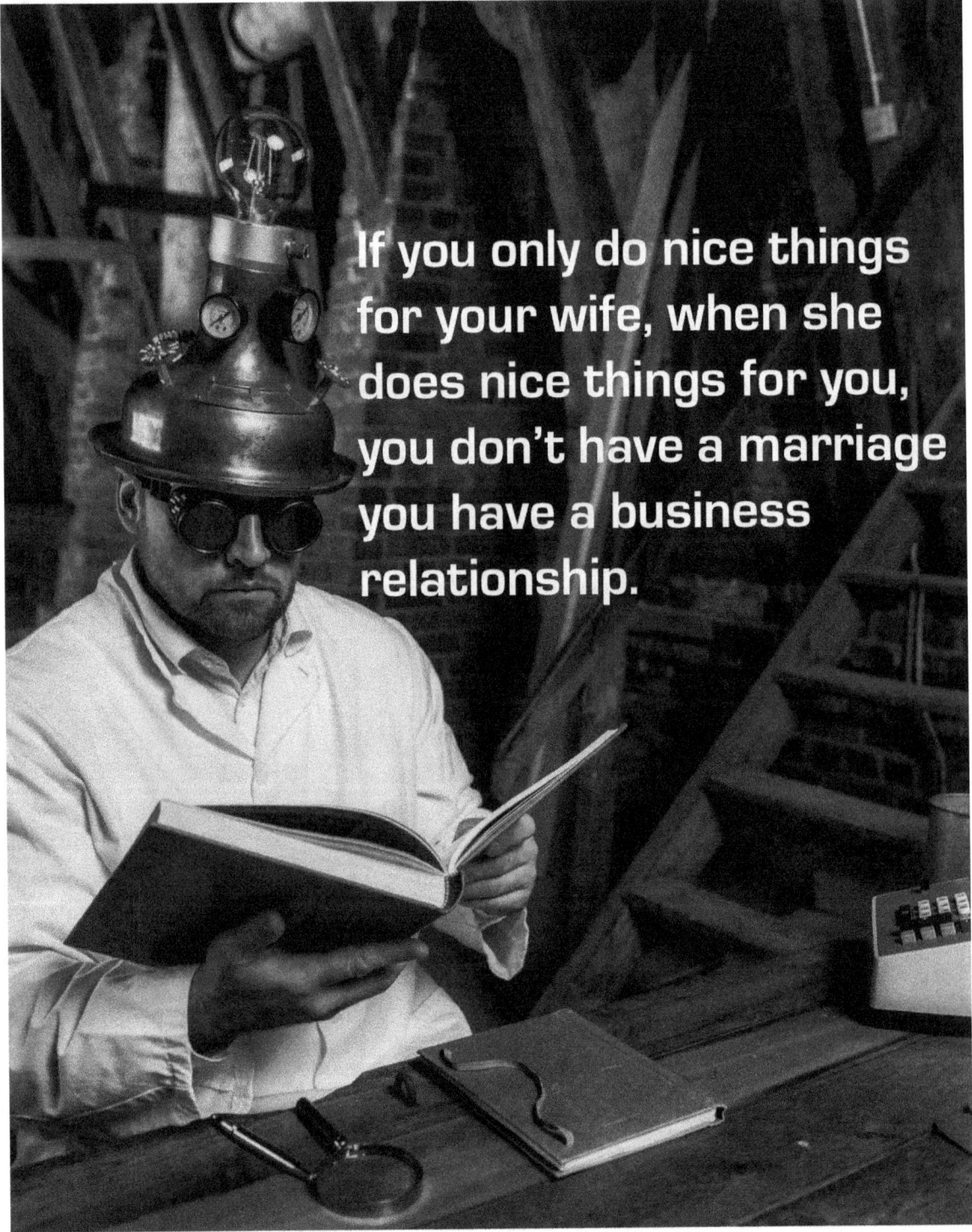

If you only do nice things for your wife, when she does nice things for you, you don't have a marriage you have a business relationship.

If you cannot speak
words to lift your wife up,
it would be best to simply
shut up.

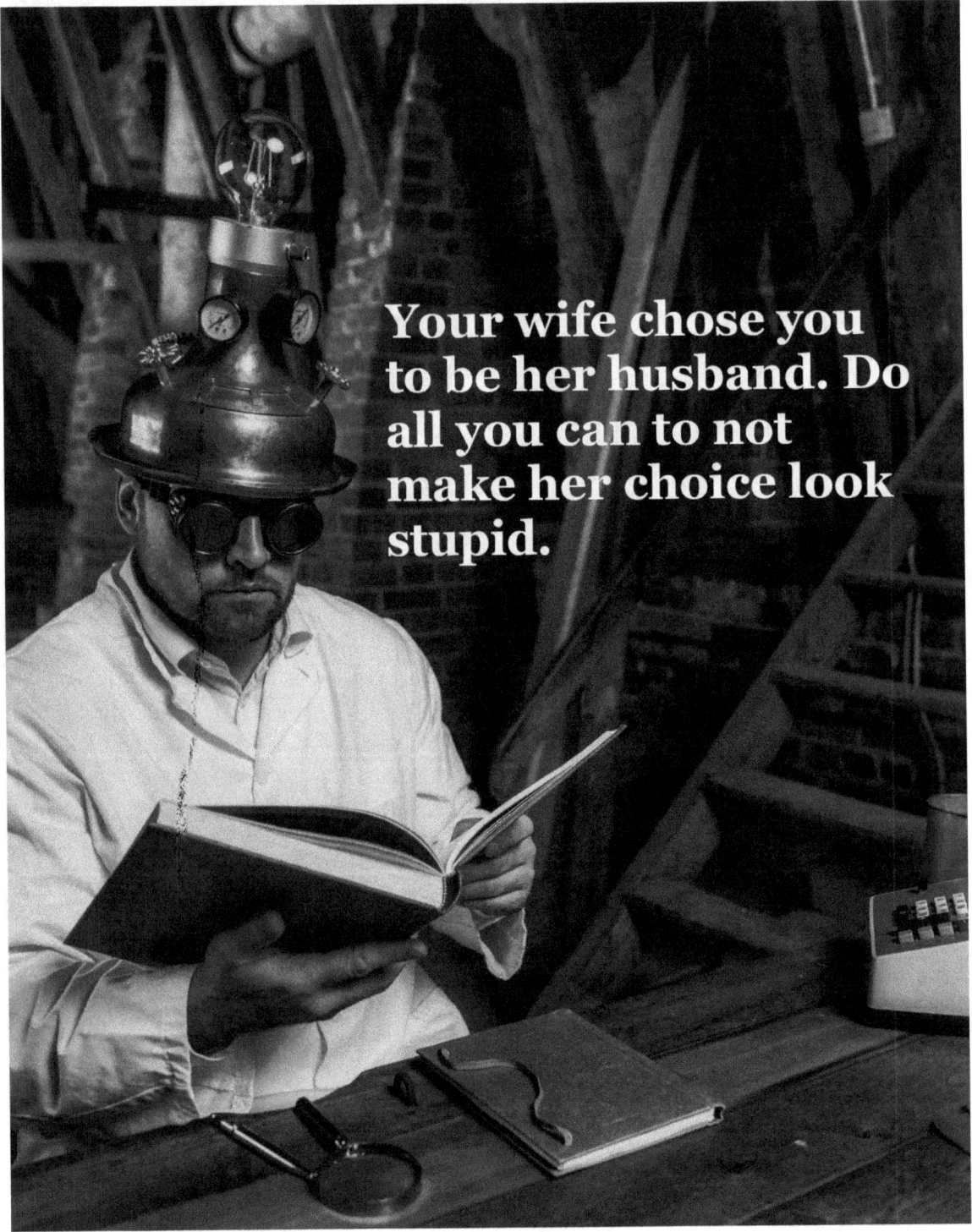

Your wife chose you to be her husband. Do all you can to not make her choice look stupid.

It takes real commitment
to keep a commitment.

Before you speak to your wife, remember that every word you say will either bring you closer or divide you further.

If you treat your wife like trash, one day someone will come by and pick her up.

Count to ten before saying something stupid. If that isn't enough to stop you, keep counting until it is.

You cannot truly serve
G-D, while not serving
your wife and children.

You will never become more important by making your wife feel less important.

Be the husband that you would want your daughter to marry.

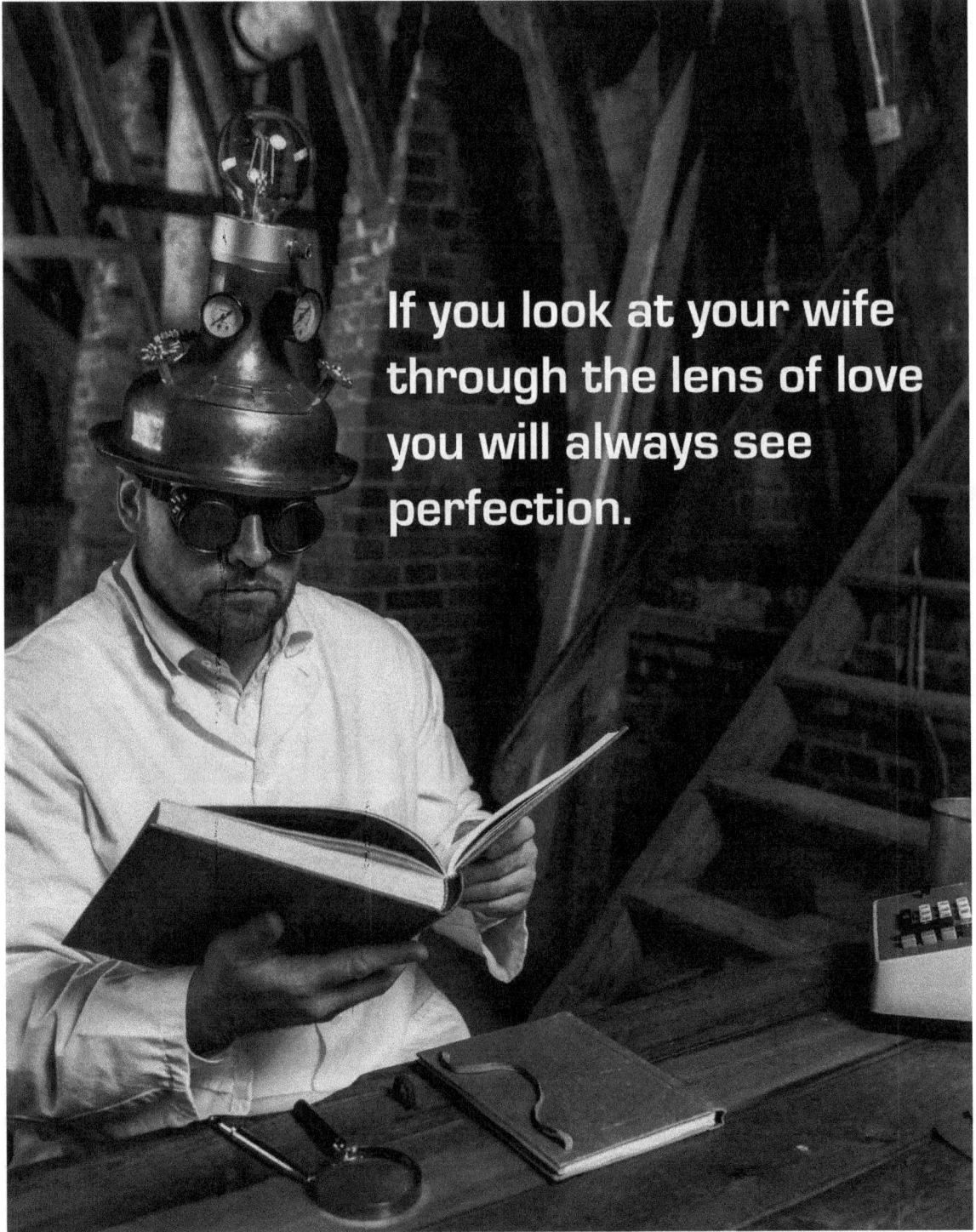

If you look at your wife
through the lens of love
you will always see
perfection.

The question isn't are you leading your wife and children?
The question is where are you leading them?

Never deceive yourself
into believing that you
know what your wife
is thinking.

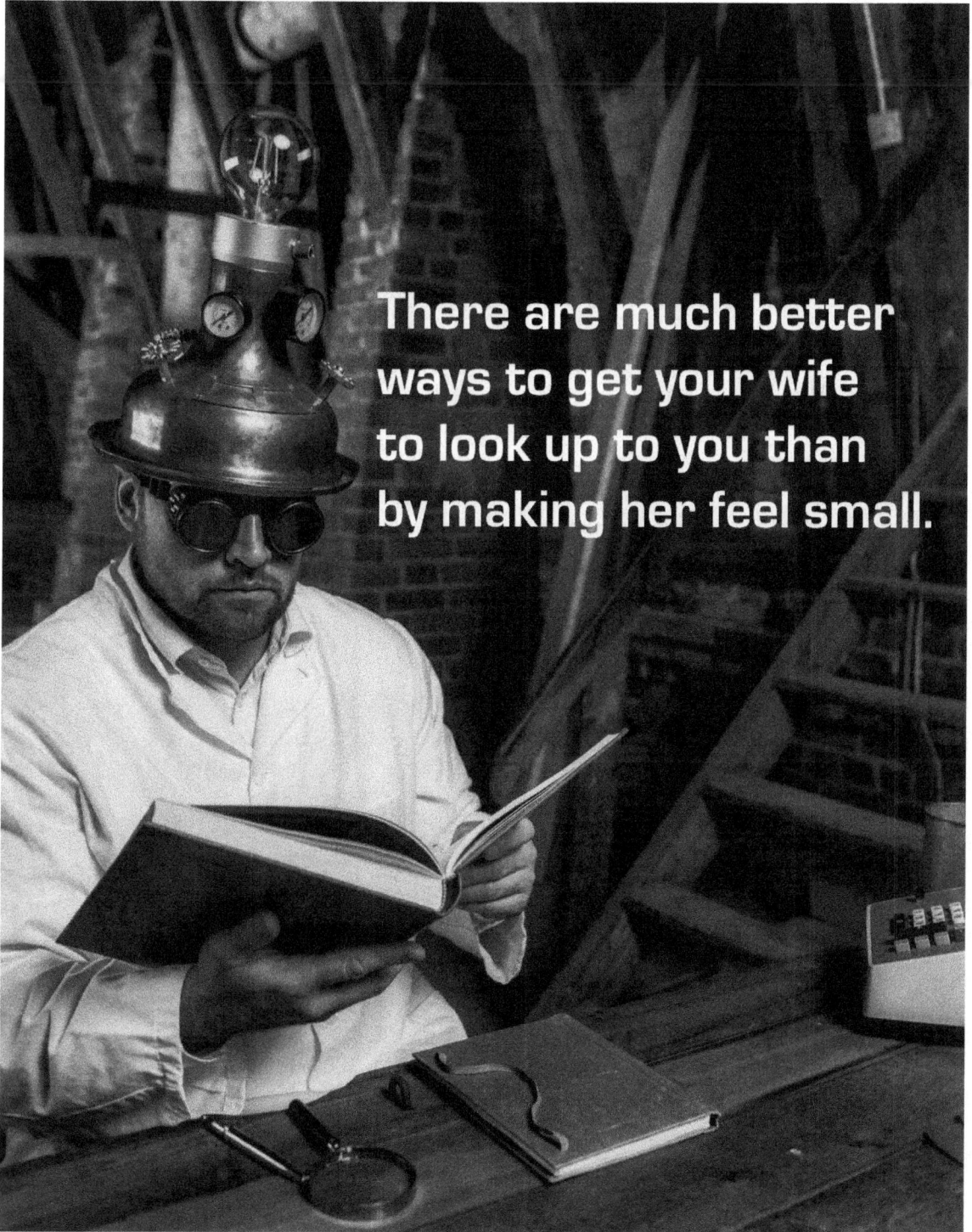

There are much better ways to get your wife to look up to you than by making her feel small.

While you may not always agree on everything, you must always agree on each other.

Respect and manners are not the fruit of a relationship, they are the seeds of one.

Work very hard to be
the husband and father
your children believe
you to be.

If you don't pray together with your wife, everything else you do together will be less.

Being honest is more than just telling the truth, it is telling the whole truth.

Don't boast that you would lay down your life for your wife, if you are not willing to lay down your will for her.

True love only
truly exists within
a commitment.

Real love is expressed through value demonstrated, not through words spoken.

Praying for your wife daily, will make you a better husband daily.

If your wife is not the most valuable thing in your home, start getting rid of things until she is.

If you want to be treated like a king you must treat your wife like a queen.

People always say;
"Love G-D, then your
wife, and then your
children." This is
incorrect because it
is impossible to love
G-D, unless you love
your wife and children.

You wife doesn't expect you to be perfect but she does expect you to be perfectly hers.

The way to be a
good husband is to
live out every promise
you vowed at your
wedding.

Prayer and praise are the oil that keepsyour marriage running smoothly.

There is a big difference between demanding your wife's submission and deserving your wife's submission.

Your wife displayed a huge amount of confidence in you when she said yes, do everything in your power to prove her correct.

Marriage is the commitment of a 100% investment, an investment of any less than 100% is a premeditated decision to fail.

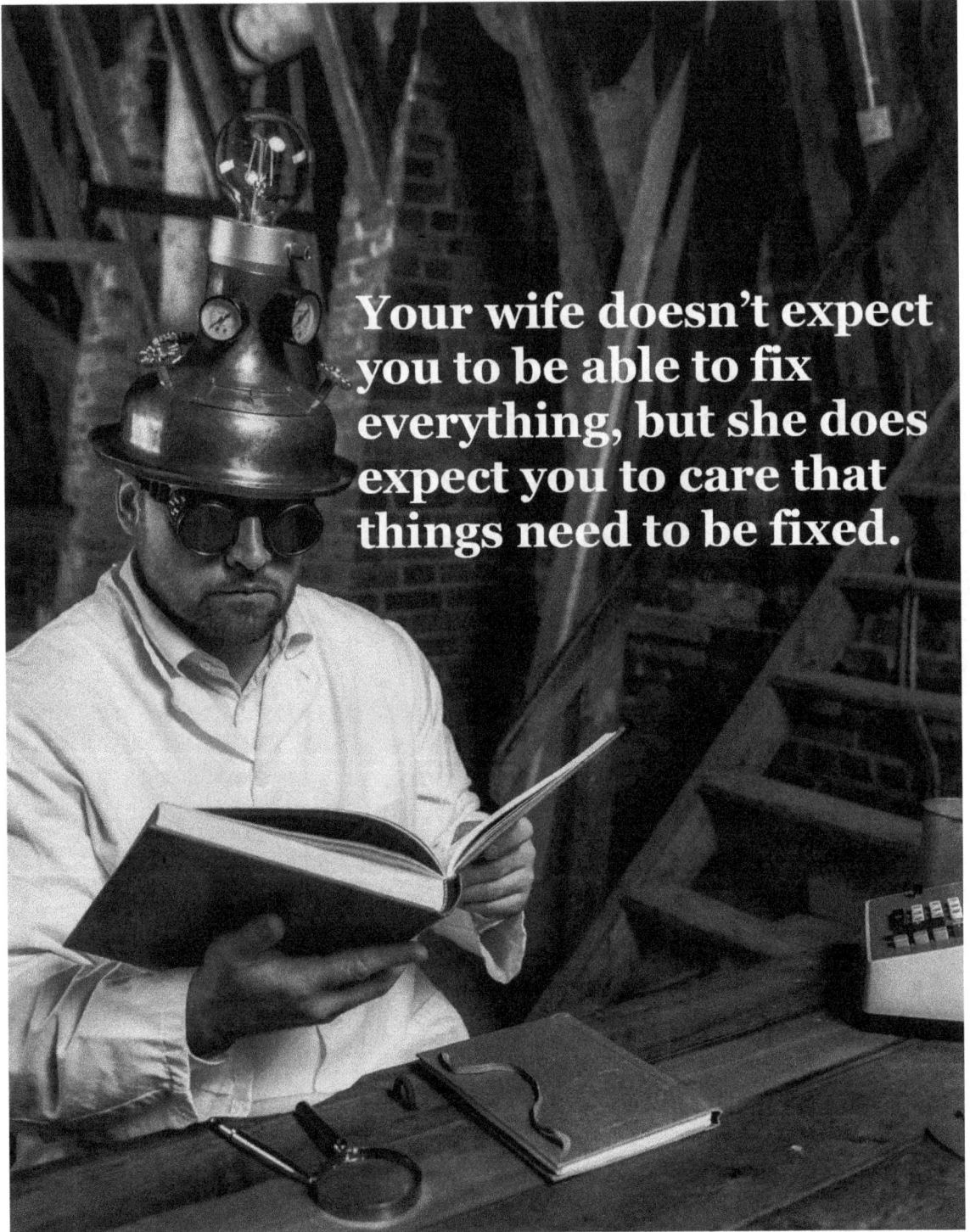

Your wife doesn't expect you to be able to fix everything, but she does expect you to care that things need to be fixed.

A great husband, is a man who is a good husband, no matter the circumstances.

You should treat your wife so well, that she spends more time praying for you, than she spends praying about you.

Listening to your wife
may not always
solve every problem
but it will keep from
adding one more
problem to the pile.

It is just as important to know when not to speak as it is to know what to say.

There are times when your wife needs a hug more than she needs a lecture.

For my wife of 35 years Pammy, without whom I would know none of what is contained within this book.

www.ingramcontent.com/pod-product-compliance
Lightning Source LLC
Chambersburg PA
CBHW081259040426
42452CB00014B/2568